THE
Lord
IS COME

THE
Lord
IS COME

CELEBRATING
TRADITIONS OF THE
SEASON

COLLEEN L. REECE AND
ANITA CORRINE DONIHUE

BARBOUR
PUBLISHING, INC.
Uhrichsville, Ohio

Published by Barbour Publishing, Inc., P.O. Box 719, Uhrichsville, OH 44683 http://www.barbourbooks.com

ecpa Member of the
Evangelical Christian
Publishers Association

Printed in the United States of America.

CONTENTS

PART 1
THANKSGIVING

"COME, YE THANKFUL
PEOPLE, COME"

Come, ye thankful people, come,
Raise the song of harvest home.
All is safely gathered in
Ere the winter storms begin;
God, our Maker, doth provide
For our wants to be supplied;
Come to God's own temple, come,
Raise the song of harvest home.

HENRY ALFORD (1810–1871)

BLESSINGS ARE WHERE
YOU FIND THEM

Freedom. The Pilgrims came to America seeking the blessing of religious freedom. They paid a high price, losing almost half their original number the first winter. We owe much to those who refused to bow before any king but God. They opened the way for the freedom of worship we often take for granted.

Happiness. Pollyanna, beloved heroine of the children's classic, received the richest heritage of all from her impoverished minister father: the ability to recognize blessings. She clung to the promise, "All things work together for good to them that love God. . ." (Romans 8:28) and found joy in doing so.

Family and friends. "Over the river, and through the woods, to Grandmother's house we go" conjures up images of horse-drawn sleighs filled with excited, laughing families. Most of us don't go to Grandmother's house by sleigh, but the same thrill of anticipation surges through us. Who will be there? Cousins we don't often see? Newcomers who quickly become part of the warm, loving group around our table? Heads bowed, hearts light as the fragrant, flickering candles, we give thanks for the priceless blessing of family and friends.

THE TRUE
THANKSGIVING

"Not what we give, but what we share,—
For the gift without the giver is bare;
Who gives himself with his alms feeds three,—
Himself, his hungering neighbor and Me."

from "The Vision of Sir Launfal,"
JAMES RUSSELL LOWELL (1819–1891)

Roger had a gnawing feeling he needed to do something for his neighbors for Thanksgiving. Mr. Smith had lost his job. He, his wife, and little girl were being evicted from their apartment because they couldn't pay the rent.

What could Roger do? He discussed the problem with his wife and children in a family meeting. "How would you like to make this Thanksgiving the most meaningful ever?" he asked. "We have a chance to open our hearts and home and give the Smiths a true Thanksgiving."

"Yes!" came the unanimous vote.

Roger immediately invited their neighbors to Thanksgiving dinner. He assisted the Smiths in finding help from local churches and community centers. Roger and his family squeezed their own tight budget to add to the growing fund.

Thanksgiving arrived. Only a few days remained until the end of the month and the fund was one hundred desperately needed dollars short. The Smiths would be forced to move. The two families circled the festive table and offered thanks for God's blessings. They told God they trusted Him to meet the Smith's needs. As they began to eat, the phone rang.

Roger answered. He listened, smiled, said thank you, and came back to the table. "That was my boss," he told Mr. Smith. "I shared my concerns with him a few days ago." A broad grin creased his face. "He wants to see you at nine o'clock sharp tomorrow morning. He has a job opening, if you're interested."

"Am I!" Mr. Smith shouted, laughing and crying at the same time.

Roger laughed, too. "I already told him that." He stopped and mysteriously lowered his voice. "There's more. The employees at work took up a collection. They had no idea how much you needed but it came to $200."

The Smiths gasped. "With the other, that's enough for us to pay the rent, and buy groceries and gas."

"And," Roger reminded, "it won't be long until payday."

Two happy families continued their Thanksgiving dinner, experiencing what the holiday was really all about.

THANKSGIVING BLACKOUT

Mom and I always looked forward to Thanksgiving. Not just as a prelude to Christmas, but as a day set apart to express our appreciation to the Lord. One unforgettable year we were invited to join my sister-in-law's family celebration. We'd leave about noon for the hour's drive to their home north of Seattle.

A wild storm swept through the area and knocked out power. By midmorning, we wondered if we'd be going anywhere. Families with partially cooked turkeys panicked. Others huddled inside their homes, complaining and wondering how long the blackout would last.

Our family is a hardy bunch of souls, rarely kept home by weather. "We'll finish cooking on the gas barbeque," was the word from our host, hostesses, and girls. "We won't be able to watch the special video we purchased, but we'll have a great time, anyway."

We did! We ate by candlelight. Later, the kids curled up at Mom's feet, enthralled by her stories from "the olden days" (she was born in 1896 and lived until 1992). We laughed and visited, experiencing the simple joy of being together. The lack of power changed from inconvenience to opportunity and the day became one of our most memorable and enjoyable Thanksgivings.

A GIFT OF THANKSGIVING

Kelly did *not* want to work at the restaurant on Thanksgiving. She had last-minute touches to put on her own meal. Her husband and children impatiently waited for her to come home. "Not until 4:00 P.M.," she sighed. "Some Thanksgiving."

The day went smoothly but dragged until 3:00 P.M. A cold draft came from the doorway. An elderly man shuffled in, silvery head bent low. He sat down.

"Why, Mr. Wilson!" Kelly smiled at him. "I haven't seen you for months. You used to be a regular customer. Happy Thanksgiving."

"My wife died of a heart attack." He spoke haltingly and his chin quivered. "I hoped you'd be open. I didn't want to spend Thanksgiving alone."

"We're glad you came." Kelly quickly told the other employees what had happened. They brought Mr. Wilson a grand meal, gave him a discount and took turns stopping at his table to visit, listen, and share amusing restaurant news.

Kelly apologized for having to leave at the end of her shift, but Sherry came on and took over. Mr. Wilson sat smiling, shoulders squared and head high. When Kelly told him to come back soon, he jauntily replied, "I will. I just can't stay away from such nice friends." Kelly drove home, warm inside, thankful for the Thanksgiving gift she had both given and received.

"GIVE THANKS"

O give thanks, give thanks unto the Lord,
For He is good, and His mercy endureth forever.
To Him which led His people through the
    wilderness,
For He is good, and His mercy endureth forever.
He turned the wilderness into a standing water,
And dry ground into water springs.
Strengthen ye the weak hands and confirm the
    feeble knees,
Say to them that are of a fearful heart,
Be strong, fear not, behold your God will
    come with a recompense.
Then shall the eyes of the blind be opened
And the ears of the deaf, of the deaf unstoppèd.
And a highway shall be there,
And it shall be called the way, the way of holiness,
The unclean shall not pass over it,
The unclean shall not pass over it,
But the redeemèd of the Lord shall walk therein;
And the ransomed of the Lord shall return and
    come to Zion,
To Zion with songs and everlasting joy upon
    their heads,
They shall obtain joy and gladness,
And sorrow and sighing shall flee away.

Words & Music: Unknown; appeared in
Shaker Hymnal (East Canterbury, New
Hampshire: The Canterbury Shakers, 1906)

"THANKS TO GOD"

Thanks to God for my Redeemer,
  Thanks for all Thou dost provide!
Thanks for times now but a mem'ry,
  Thanks for Jesus by my side!
Thanks for pleasant, balmy springtime,
  Thanks for dark and stormy fall!
Thanks for tears by now forgotten,
  Thanks for peace within my soul!

Thanks for prayers that Thou hast answered,
  Thanks for what Thou dost deny!
Thanks for storms that I have weathered,
  Thanks for all Thou dost supply!
Thanks for pain, and thanks for pleasure,
  Thanks for comfort in despair!
Thanks for grace that none can measure,
  Thanks for love beyond compare!

Thanks for roses by the wayside,
  Thanks for thorns their stems contain!
Thanks for home and thanks for fireside,
  Thanks for hope, that sweet refrain!
Thanks for joy and thanks for sorrow,
  Thanks for heavenly peace with Thee!
Thanks for hope in the tomorrow,
  Thanks through all eternity!

AUGUST LUDVIG STORM, 1862–1914

THANKFUL FOR LIFE

Thanksgiving finally came. Although not all her family could be together, Gloria still felt happy. Some would be there for dinner; she and her husband Frank would talk with the others by phone. Son Joe, his wife Sandy, and their two children lived in eastern Washington. Eight months pregnant, Sandy couldn't make the trip over the pass to Seattle. The freeway was solid ice.

Another thoughtful son and daughter-in-law were sending flowers. Gloria thrilled at how they'd adorn her table. With dinner underway, she turned things down and hurried to the store for last-minute items. Back home, she wheeled into the driveway and jostled open the door. Where was Frank?

His voice trailed from the nearby study. "We don't know if he's conscious or how serious it is, but we'll keep you posted."

"What's wrong?" She carried the groceries to the kitchen.

"Joe, Sandy, and the kids have been in a five-car pileup."

Gloria dropped the groceries, grabbed Frank's hand and they began to pray. They had seen God work many times through the years. He could go the miles to help their beloved family. Gloria called the other children, told them what had happened and canceled dinner. She shoved food in the refrigerator and threw a few things in a suitcase. Just before they left, the flowers arrived. Gloria gazed at them through wet eyes and placed them in a cool room.

The trip took forever. Gloria's thoughts whirred with the car's engine hum. Was Joe conscious? The children were bruised and frightened. How were Sandy and her unborn baby? Finally they wheeled into the hospital parking lot.

Joe had received a head injury; he slipped in and out of consciousness. Sandy was bruised completely down one side, had a dislocated shoulder and had gone into labor. The grandchildren hovered near, confused. Yet others in the accident had been injured far more seriously.

After several hours, Joe and the children were released. Frank and Gloria watched all night to make sure he wouldn't slip into a coma.

The next day, Sandy's labor stopped. The baby's vital signs were good, so she went home but could not care for the children. Frank and Gloria took them back to Seattle. On the way, snow flew in the cold night air, visibility so terrible that Frank drove by the white line on the road. The children quietly slept in the back seat. Once they were across the pass, they'd never been so happy to see rain.

"What a Thanksgiving this has been," Gloria whispered.

Frank stopped at a traffic light and gazed at his wife with a smile. "Yes," he said. "What a Thanksgiving to be thankful for life."

"THE WORLD IS MINE"

Today, upon a bus, I saw a lovely girl with
    golden hair.
I envied her, she seemed so bright; I wished I
    were as fair.
When suddenly she rose to leave, I saw her
    hobble down the aisle;
She had one leg, and wore a crutch, and as she
    passed—a smile.
O God, forgive me when I whine;
I have two legs. The world is mine.

And when I stopped to buy some sweets, the
    lad who sold them had such charm.
I talked with him—he seemed so glad—if we
    were late 'twould do no harm.
And as I left he said to me, "I thank you. You
    have been so kind.
It's nice to talk with folks like you. You see,"
    he said. "I'm blind."
O God, forgive me when I whine.
I have two eyes. The world is mine.

Later, walking down the street, I saw a child
    with eyes of blue.
He stood and watched the others play; it
    seemed he knew not what to do.
I stopped a moment, then I said: "Why don't
    you join the others, dear?"
He looked ahead without a word, and then I
    knew—he could not hear.
O God, forgive me when I whine.
I have two ears. The world is mine.

With legs to take me where I'd go,
With eyes to see the sunset's glow,
With ears to hear what I would know.
O God, forgive me when I whine.
I'm blessed indeed. The world is mine.

AUTHOR UNKNOWN

I have learned, in whatsoever state I am,
therewith to be content.
PHILIPPIANS 4:11

A Shovel, a Smile,

and a Loaf of Bread

Lars peered through the curtain toward a neighbor's house. "Funny, Mrs. Cooper hasn't come out lately. Wonder if she's all right?"

Wendy pulled loaves of homemade bread from the oven. *They'd be just right for the church Thanksgiving basket that would go to a needy family,* she thought.

"I just don't feel good about this," her husband went on. "Not even a trip to the mailbox. There would be tracks in the snow." He turned to Wendy. "I'm going to check on her." He shrugged into his heavy coat and went out.

Wendy glanced at the clock, then out the window. Lars had already begun shoveling Mrs. Cooper's walk. "Two hours until time to leave for church," she murmured. "I'll have time to make a couple more loaves of bread."

Later, Lars and Wendy took the bread and a rice casserole to Mrs. Cooper.

"How wonderful!" she croaked. "I've been sick with the flu and couldn't get to the store. Not that it mattered. I haven't felt like cooking. Thank you so much."

Wendy hugged her. "You're part of the family. We'll check again tomorrow."

Lars and Wendy headed for church. "Do you have the Thanksgiving basket?" he asked.

She nodded. "Yes, but I'm glad God reminded us charity begins at home."

PART 2:
THE WONDER OF WINTER

"THE FIRST SNOWFALL"

The snow had begun in the gloaming,
And busily all the night
Had been heaping field and highway
With a silence deep and white.

Every pine and fir and hemlock
Wore ermine too dear for an earl,
And the poorest twig on the elm-tree
Was ridged inch-deep with pearl.

From sheds new-roofed with Carrara*
Came Chanticleer's muffled crow,
The stiff rails were softened to swan's-down,
And still fluttered down the snow.

I stood and watched by the window
The noiseless work of the sky,
And the sudden flurries of snow-birds
Like brown leaves whirling by.

Up spoke our own little Mabel,
Saying, "Father, who makes it snow?"
And I told of the good All-father
Who cares for us here below.

And again to the child I whispered,
"The snow that husheth all,
Darling, the merciful Father
Alone can make it fall!"

JAMES RUSSELL LOWELL (1819–1891)

* *The marble of Carrara, Italy, is noted for its
   purity.*

THE MAGIC

OF THE SINGLE SNOWFLAKE

If you have lost your sense of wonder,
the mystical awe a single snowflake brings,
you have lost much.

One snowflake often heralds a storm.
So what? You cannot stop the snow from
sifting down to cover the barren, waiting earth.

Return to the magic of childhood,
The rebirth of wonder.
Warm your heart and hands
at the blaze of your children's gaze.

Then remember a day long ago,
when you, too,
thanked God for the snow.

SLEDS AND SLEDDING

Growing up near the small, western Washington logging town of Darrington meant making snow our friend, not an enemy. People worked together. Night after night, we awakened to the sound of a tractor equipped with a snow plow as neighbor helped neighbor, digging out driveways. We also prided ourselves on the ability to adapt. We got more snow than most nearby towns, but our schools stayed open when theirs shut down for a few accumulated inches.

Winter fun wasn't just for kids. Each evening half the town gathered to pack slopes into great ski and sled runs. Bobsleds abounded. Some were wagon beds mounted on runners and drawn by trucks, Jeeps or cars.

One winter, my uncle hitched up a bobsled with several of us aboard. Over the packed roads we rode, taking turns and laughing when seventy-something Mom joined us. My young nephew got a bright idea. He tied his small sled to the back of the bobsled and away we went up and down the hilly road. Suddenly a bellow came out of the darkness behind us. "Wait for me!" A bump had freed his sled "caboose," sent him flying, and left him sliding backwards down the road.

I never see a snowfall without cherishing these memories.

DOG SLED

Now that I live in the suburbs, I can't go bob-sledding. I do, however, enjoy watching the kids sled on the street next to my place. The bolder ones climb to the top, push off and go kicking and yelling down to the intersection. There they steer hard left and safely speed down, down, down to the end of the cul-de-sac.

A few weeks ago, three or four inches of per-fect packing snow fell. After school, kids rushed out in droves. Then came a Norman Rockwell moment. A perfectly positioned sled waited in the middle of the intersection. All alone, in the exact center of the sled, a black and white springer spaniel sat, ready to be pushed off. The expression on the dog's face showed two things: (1) it obviously wasn't his first trip, and (2) he was enjoying himself immensely!

All the world's sophisticated toys and games can never compete with the old-fashioned fun of snowpeople and sledding. Just ask my neighbors (and their good-sport spaniel) who coast on my hill every time God blesses us with a few inches of the wonderful white stuff called snow.

PART 3:

FIT FOR THE KING

KEEPING FIT

"Do you not know that your body is a temple of the Holy Spirit, who is in you, whom you have received from God? You are not your own; you were bought at a price. Therefore honor God with your body" (1 Corinthians 6:19–20, NIV).

One of the joys of the holiday season is food. "A time to indulge," some call it. Cookie-baking, candy-making, and lavish meals play havoc with carefully established eating habits, to say nothing of diets! Too much rich food extracts a price: lethargy, headaches, stomach distress, even lowered resistance to viruses floating around in the winter air.

It's easy to become a temporary couch potato over the holidays. Keeping fit for the King, both physically and spiritually, requires planning. We can honor Him with our bodies by monitoring the amount of junk food we consume, making sure we exercise and sleep properly, and concentrating on the Spirit of Christmas, rather than the keeping of the day.

A WISER WAY

Every year just before Thanksgiving, three rob-bers—Stress, Impress and Depress—turn up on our doorsteps. Programs and parties, gift-buying and goody-making, late hours, and lack of normal routine leave us exhausted.

Taking steps to confront and overcome the inharmonious "ess" trio helps welcome the Guest of Honor at His birthday party as He deserves. He's the only one we need to impress. Why let stress lead to depression and (too often) secret relief when what should be a "holy-day" season is over?

Quick Tips to a "Holy-Day" Season

* Take a brisk walk every day, even if it's only for ten minutes.
* Remember whose birthday Christmas is. Act accordingly.
* Consider going out for Thanksgiving or Christmas dinner.
* Consider purchasing the traditional turkey dinner at a local supermarket deli.
* Consider using the new fluffy canned biscuits instead of homemade rolls.
* A pretty table brightens even a soup-and-sandwich meal.
* An elegant dessert enhances simple meals.
* Keep desserts after heavy meals light and fluffy.

The following tested recipes offer healthful ways to eat well with little fuss.

OLD-FASHIONED
CLAM CHOWDER
A good Christmas Eve tradition.

½ cup chopped bacon or salt pork
½ cup chopped celery and onion
Four large diced potatoes
1 tablespoon chopped parsley (fresh or dried)
Chicken broth, enough to cover vegetables
One large can clams (rinsed, reserving juice)
3½ cups skim milk
1 tablespoon butter or margarine
Dash paprika
Salt and pepper to taste
1 teaspoon corn starch
½ cup milk

In a saucepan, combine bacon, celery, onion, parsley, and chicken broth and butter. Bring to a boil, reduce heat, and cover, simmering until vegetables are tender. Add clams, milk, and seasonings. Heat through but do not boil. Combine cornstarch and ½ cup milk. Add to soup and stir until thickened. Garnish with fresh parsley.

CROWD-PLEASER PLATTER

Greet your guests with a colorful alternative to candy and nuts. Choose a variety of fruit and vegetables, displaying them to make the best use of color and texture. Chop and slice ahead of time, storing each item in a separate container until just before serving time.

Broccoli flowerets	Dill pickles
Baby carrots	Sliced cucumbers
Assorted olives	Radishes
Cherry tomatoes	Celery sticks
Cauliflower flowerets	

Arrange with a variety of crackers and cheese, and serve with your favorite dip. Or try the dill dip recipe below. Also include fruit, such as pineapple, banana, apple, orange, and strawberries.

Dill Dip

1 cup sour cream	1 cup mayonnaise
1 tablespoon dill	1 tablespoon minced
1 teaspoon garlic salt	onion

Mix well, and chill for at least 1 hour before serving. Garnish with chopped red pepper for a splash of color.

PASTA PIE

This easy-to-make pie tastes like lasagna. Make ahead and freeze for later.

1 pound ground beef, chicken, or turkey
One jar spaghetti sauce
2 tablespoons butter or margarine
⅓ cup Parmesan cheese
1 egg, beaten
8 ounces cooked pasta, such as spaghetti, angel hair, or linguine
12 ounces cottage cheese
2 cups shredded Mozzarella cheese

Preheat oven to 350 degrees. Brown and drain meat. Add spaghetti sauce, butter, Parmesan, and beaten egg. Mix well. Spread pasta in a 9x13-inch pan. Spread cottage cheese evenly over pasta, followed by meat mixture. Bake for 30 minutes. Top with Mozzarella and bake 10 minutes longer.

Let stand 5–10 minutes before serving. Top with Parmesan cheese (optional). Cut into squares to serve.

PUMPKIN PUDDING

Pumpkin pie is an all-time holiday favorite. It is also high in fat and cholesterol. Surprise your family this year with this delicious pumpkin pudding that eliminates the crust and uses non-fat milk in the filling! (You may wish to double the recipe.)

Two eggs, beaten
One 16-ounce can pumpkin
½ cup brown sugar
½ teaspoon salt
1 teaspoon ground ginger
¼ teaspoon ground cloves
1¼ cups nonfat milk

Preheat oven to 425 degrees. Mix all ingredients in a medium bowl. Pour into a 8x8-inch square pan. Bake 15 minutes, then reduce oven heat to 350 degrees. Bake 40 to 50 minutes, or until knife inserted near center comes out clean.

Serve slightly warm or cold, offering whipped topping or ice cream alongside.

EDINBURGH GINGERBREAD

4 cups flour
¼ teaspoon salt
1½ teaspoons ginger
1½ teaspoons cinnamon
1½ teaspoons mixed spice
½ teaspoon cloves
1 cup pitted dates, chopped coarsely
1 cup walnuts, chopped coarsely
1 cup butter or margarine
1 cup molasses
1 cup packed brown sugar
4 eggs, beaten
1 teaspoon baking soda
1–2 teaspoons warm milk

Mix together flour, salt, spices, dates, and walnuts. Melt butter, molasses, and sugar over low heat. Pour mixture gradually over flour mixture, stirring well. Beat in eggs. Dissolve baking soda in warm milk and add to mixture. Stir well with a wooden spoon, adding more milk if dough is too stiff. Pour batter into a greased and lined 8-inch square pan. Bake at 350 degrees for 20 minutes. Lower temperature to 300 degrees and bake for another 2 hours.

CRANBERRY SALAD SUPREME

3-ounce package raspberry gelatin
1 cup boiling water
16-ounce can whole cranberry sauce
3-ounce package lemon gelatin
1 cup boiling water
3-ounce package cream cheese
⅓ cup mayonnaise
8-ounce can crushed pineapple
½ cup whipped cream
1 cup miniature marshmallows
2 tablespoons chopped nuts

Dissolve raspberry gelatin in a cup boiling water. Stir in whole cranberry sauce. Turn into 9x9x2-inch baking dish. Chill until partially set. Dissolve lemon gelatin in 1 cup boiling water. Beat together cream cheese and mayonnaise, then gradually add lemon gelatin. Stir in undrained pineapple. Chill until partially set. Add whipped cream; fold in lemon mixture and marshmallows. Spread on top of cranberry layer. Top with chopped nuts. Chill until firmly set.

SWEET POTATO CASSEROLE

1 large can sweet potatoes
¾ cup sugar
2 eggs
1 teaspoon vanilla
1 stick margarine, melted
½ cup evaporated milk

Topping:
1 cup brown sugar
⅓ cup flour
1 cup chopped nuts
⅓ cup margarine

Mash potatoes with juice. Mix all ingredients with potatoes and pour into greased 9x13-inch pan. Mix topping ingredients until crumbly and sprinkle on top of mixture. Do not stir. Bake at 350 degrees for about 40 minutes.

CORN CASSEROLE

1-pound can whole kernel corn
1-pound can cream style corn
8 ounces sour cream (or 1 cup milk)
1 egg, beaten
3 tablespoons chopped onion
1 small box quick corn muffin mix
½ stick margarine
½ teaspoon parsley
½ teaspoon salt
½ teaspoon pepper

Combine all ingredients. Bake at 350 degrees in greased 7x11-inch casserole dish for 45 minutes. Serves 10.

HOLIDAY CRACKERS

16 ounces plain oyster crackers
1 package ranch dressing dry mix
¼–½ teaspoon lemon pepper seasoning
½–1 teaspoon dill weed
¼–½ teaspoon garlic powder
¾–1 cup salad oil or olive oil

Combine ranch dressing mix and oil; add dill weed, garlic powder, and lemon pepper. Pour over crackers, stir well to coat. Place in warm oven for 20 minutes. Stir well halfway through. Place in airtight container.

CORN MUFFINS

1½ cups yellow cornmeal
½ cup all-purpose flour
2 tablespoons granulated sugar
2 teaspoons baking powder
½ teaspoon baking soda
½ teaspoon salt
1¼ cups buttermilk
¼ cup unsweetened applesauce
2 egg whites
2 tablespoons vegetable oil

In large bowl combine first six ingredients. Combine buttermilk, applesauce, egg whites, and oil. Stir into dry ingredients, just to moisten well. Fill greased or "PAMmed" muffin cups ⅔ full. Bake at 400 degrees for 18–20 minutes. Cool in pan 8–10 minutes.

JULEKAGE (CHRISTMAS BREAD)

2 cakes or packages of yeast
1 cup milk (¾ cup milk and ¼ cup water if
   dry yeast is used instead of cake yeast)
½ cup sugar
2 eggs, slightly beaten
1 teaspoon salt
6 cardamom seeds, ground
4 cups flour
¼ cup butter
⅔ package candied fruit
black raisins
white raisins

Powdered sugar frosting:
3 cups powdered sugar
⅓ cup soft butter
1½ teaspoons almond flavoring
2 tablespoons milk

Scald and cool milk. When milk is lukewarm, dissolve yeast in milk. Mix in sugar, slightly beaten eggs, salt, cardamom, and two cups flour. Melt butter and add to mixture. Mix well. Add remaining flour, but keep dough "sticky." Mix in candied fruit and a good handful each of black and white raisins, packing in as much fruit as the mixture will hold. Knead on floured board until smooth. Put into a greased bowl to raise. (Dough should rise to twice its original size. Due to the fruit, this can take 2 hours or longer.) After dough is risen, cut it down with a knife while it is in bowl, instead of punching or kneading. Let rise again, about 45 minutes. Divide dough into two parts and pound down. Shape into loaves and let rise to about twice its size again. Bread can be baked in bread pans or formed into round loaves and baked on a greased cookie sheet or in a greased pie pan. Bake 30–40 minutes at 350 degrees.

Frosting: Cream together sugar and butter. Stir in flavoring and add milk, until desired consistency is reached.

EASIEST IMAGINABLE
HOT SPICED PUNCH

A surefire way to warm visitors and win praise.

Two to four cans frozen orange-pinneapple-
 banana blend fruit juice
A few cinnamon sticks
Some whole cloves
Thin horizontal slices of a large washed
 orange, with skin on

Follow directions for reconstituting juice. Add
cinnamon, cloves, and orange slices. Let simmer at least 30 minutes so flavors will blend.

Remove spices; leave orange slices floating.

EGGNOG

4 eggs, separated
½ cup sugar
2 cups cold milk
1 cup cold light cream
1½ teaspoons vanilla
⅛ teaspoon salt
¼ teaspoon nutmeg

Beat egg yolks together with ¼ cup sugar until thick. Gradually mix in milk, cream, vanilla, salt, and ⅛ teaspoon nutmeg, beating until frothy. Beat egg whites with remaining sugar until it forms soft peaks, then fold into egg yolk mixture. Cover and chill. Mix well before serving and sprinkle with remaining nutmeg.

MULLED CIDER

Simmer 2 quarts apple cider and 1½ cups sugar in a large pan. Add the following ingredients tied up in a cloth bag:

2 teaspoons whole allspice
5 cinnamon sticks
2 teaspoons whole cloves

Simmer for 20 minutes covered, then remove the spice bag and discard. Add:

4 cups cranberry juice
1 cup lemon juice
2 cups orange juice

Simmer another 15 minutes. Garnish with orange and lemon slices and serve hot.

ORANGE SPICED TEA

1 cup powdered orange drink mix
1 heaping cup lemon instant tea
  (unsweetened)
3 cups sugar (or equal amount of sugar
  substitute)
1 teaspoon cinnamon
½ teaspoon nutmeg (can substitute cloves)

Mix all ingredients together. Put 3 heaping tea-spoons of mix to one medium mug of hot water (boiling water is best). Use more or less to suit your taste.

HOT CHOCOLATE

1-pound can Quik, or powdered chocolate
  drink mix
1 pound sugar
8-quart box powdered sugar
3- to 6-ounce jar powdered creamer

Sift all ingredients together and store in container. Put 4 heaping teaspoons in cup of boiling water.

BUSY GRANDMA

Marcia felt the holidays closing in on her and she didn't like it. She put in long hours on her job. Now only a few days remained until her two grown children and their families came from out of town.

"I want this to be a perfect holiday," she said, busily planning menus. Yet deep inside, she already felt exhausted and frustrated. A quiet little voice began to speak to her. She stopped what she was doing and listened. Wouldn't her family rather have a rested, happy Mom to visit with than one worn out from providing the traditional elaborate meals? Marcia crumpled the paper and started over, planning dishes from quick, simple, but delicious recipes.

"Hmmm. Christmas Eve," she pondered. "How about starting a new family tradition—a big pot of soup, fresh veggies, and rolls? Lord, this is Your birthday. I'll make more time for us to share our love."

The families arrived. They were delighted with the new way of keeping Christmas and the extra time with Mom and Grandma. And Marcia had time to really listen to what they had to share, instead of concentrating on the kitchen.

PART 4:

CHRISTMAS JOY

"ANGELS WE HAVE HEARD ON HIGH"

Angels we have heard on high
Sweetly singing o'er the plains,
And the mountains in reply
Echoing their joyous strains.

Refrain:
Gloria, in excelsis Deo!
Gloria, in excelsis Deo!

Shepherds, why this jubilee?
Why your joyous strains prolong?
What the gladsome tidings be
Which inspire your heavenly song?

Refrain

Come to Bethlehem and see
Christ whose birth the angels sing;
Come, adore on bended knee,
Christ the Lord, the newborn King.

Refrain

JAMES CHADWICK, 1813–1882

No Way to Christmas

One of the things that most impresses me about the story Jesus told of the Samaritan who stopped to help a wounded Jew (Luke 10:30–36) is that no one expected him to do such a thing. He went far beyond the call of duty in aiding one of a race that despised his own.

Several years ago, this parable sprang to life a few days before Christmas. A family lived miles from their loved ones, far away in a tiny mountain town. Heavy snow closed the main route. The only way out was by train or down a steep and perilous logging road—and the family car wasn't working.

They got ready to catch the train, but it didn't come. At two o'clock in the morning, they learned a bridge had washed out. It would take days to repair the bridge. The family cried all night.

The next day a kind neighbor said she would take them down the snowy road. Hours later, they reached the town at the bottom where a sister waited. The truck driver father confessed, "Experienced as I am, I'm not sure I'd have done it."

The neighbor just smiled and started the long, lonely way back up the mountain, while the family who thought they had no way to Christmas rejoiced at being with their loved ones and thanked God for their neighbor.

As a man begins to live more seriously within,
he begins to live more simply without.
RALPH WALDO EMERSON (1803–1882)

"JOY TO THE WORLD!"

Joy to the world! The Lord is come;
Let earth receive her King;
Let every heart prepare Him room,
And heaven and nature sing,
And heaven and nature sing,
And heaven, and heaven and nature sing.

ISAAC WATTS (1674–1748)

HYMN NOTES

Long before Jesus was born, David the psalmist (a psalmist is one who writes a sacred song or poem to be used for worship) told people to sing, rejoice, praise, and make a joyful noise unto the Lord (see Psalm 98:4).

Many years later an English minister named Isaac Watts wrote a hymn carol that did just that. His rousing "Joy to the World" is over 270 years old.

Isaac Watts didn't write as many hymns and psalms as Charles Wesley, sometimes called "hymn writer of the ages," but he did write more than seven hundred! He often took the Old Testament psalms and turned them into Christian songs.

Two other important persons also contributed to this exciting carol. George F. Handel, famous composer of the oratorio *Messiah*, wrote the melody. Lowell Mason, first music teacher in America's public schools, did the arrangement we usually sing today.

Christians everywhere will go on singing, "Joy to the World! The Lord is come. . ." until Jesus comes back again and earth really does receive her King.

LITTLE BOY, LOST DOG

Mandy finished reading a bedtime story to her young children, Brian and Chelsie. Quiet and love filled the Christmas night. The children's new toys lay under the tree. Mandy closed the book. A soft rap sounded at the door. Mandy discovered a small boy standing in the dark and cold on her front porch.

He hesitantly peered up at her. "I–I lost my dog." He shivered. "Have you seen a little black dog?"

Brian darted to the door. "Hey, it's Jason. Come on in."

Jason shuffled in, head drooping. His gaze riveted on Brian's little red wagon under the tree. "Wow," he gasped. "That is awesome!" He looked back toward Mandy. "But I gotta find my dog."

"Well," she pondered. "I remember seeing a little black dog in the backyard earlier." She went to the sliding glass door and opened the curtain. Sure enough, two sorrowful button eyes looked back at them through the glass. A wet, black nose pressed to the pane.

Mandy hurriedly let the dog in and turned to Jason. "May I walk you and your dog home? Your parents must be worried."

He nodded. "It's just my mom. I live in the

apartments out there." He motioned toward the family's backyard.

Mandy gave her children instructions, walked Jason home and quickly returned. Brian and Chelsie climbed into bed.

Brian locked his arms behind his head and settled back on his pillow. "Jason's really poor, Mom," he said thoughtfully. "I don't think he got much for Christmas. Did you see the way he looked at my new wagon?"

Mandy nodded. "I wonder what we could do to help."

"I got some money for Christmas. Would it be enough to buy a wagon?"

Chelsie jumped up and down on her bed. "I could help with my money, too," she bubbled.

Mandy gazed at her children with pride. *And a little child shall lead them,* she thought. She felt a twinge of guilt. "My money from Grandpa and Grandma can go to make up the difference. I don't have to buy the watch I wanted."

The next day the family pooled their treasury. They had just enough to buy a wagon, because of the after-Christmas half-off sales. Brian, Mandy, and Chelsie waited until Jason wasn't home, then they slipped over with the wagon in a big box. They set it outside Jason's front door with a note that read:

"To Brian and his little black dog. Love, from a friend."

LOVE RECONCILED

A friend loveth at all times. . .
PROVERBS 17:17, KJV

No treasure has greater value than showing kindness and love to another.

Marty and Terry had been facing too much stress. Busy supporting and raising young children, they worked long hours on opposite shifts to make ends meet. They had little time together as a family and practically none for themselves. Day by day their love dwindled.

Terry's co-worker Linda saw the hurt in Terry's eyes. She grew concerned. Knowing what prayer could do, she took Terry and Marty's needs to the Lord.

Not long after, Terry came to Linda and shared her dilemma in a series of long talks. With Christmas rushing closer, the stress grew. The company had an employee gift exchange and Linda drew Terry's name. She tucked in a poem along with a small gift, then hugged Terry.

Terry read it. So did Marty. They couldn't keep back the tears.

"Don't give up," Linda pleaded.

They didn't give up. Terry and Marty renewed their pledge of never-ending love. Relatives and friends helped with the kids occasionally and the couple worked hard at tightening their budget and workload to make time together.

When the following Christmas arrived, things were far different.

"We used to eat dinner around the TV. Now," Terry glowed, "we gather at the table like a real, new family in love. This Christmas I feel like celebrating!"

And so did Linda.

"KEEP LOVING"

This is the poem Linda gave her friend.

Keep loving because of—
Keep loving in spite of—
Keep loving when to love is most difficult.
Keep loving when there's no strength.
Keep loving because Jesus loves you
   in good times and bad,
    on mountaintops, in valleys.
When all else fails,
Keep on loving.

ANITA CORRINE DONIHUE, 1995

"AWAY IN A MANGER"

Away in a manger, no crib for a bed,
The little Lord Jesus laid down His sweet
  head.
The stars in the sky looked down where
  He lay,
The little Lord Jesus, asleep on the hay.
The cattle are lowing, the Baby awakes,
But little Lord Jesus, no crying He makes;
I love Thee, Lord Jesus, look down from
  the sky
And stay by my cradle til morning is nigh.
Be near me, Lord Jesus, I ask Thee to stay
Close by me forever, and love me, I pray;
Bless all the dear children in Thy tender care,
And fit us for heaven to live with Thee there.

Verses 1 & 2, anonymous
Verse 3 is by JOHN THOMAS MCFARLAND,
1851–1913

CHILD IN THE MANGER

Child in the manger, infant of Mary,
Outcast and Stranger, Lord of us all,
Child Who inherits all our transgressions,
All our demerits upon Him fall.
Once the most holy Child of salvation
Gently and lowly lived here below.
Now as our glorious mighty Redeemer,
See Him victorious over each foe.
Prophets foretold Him, Infant of wonder;
Angels behold Him on His throne.
Worthy our Savior of all our praises;
Happy forever are His own.

LESS IS MORE

Ken had been laid off work for several months. Things got tighter and tighter. Meager monies from Ken's odd jobs and Sandra's baby-sitting barely stretched to meet their needs. With Christmas approaching, Ken and Sandra prayed hard. They asked God to make it the best Christmas ever for their three children, in spite of hard times. Somehow they managed to come up with one nice but modest gift for each child.

Sandra took Ken's hands and gazed into his eyes. "We'll concentrate on making our Christmas dinner wonderful," she assured him. "We will make less into more." She worked tirelessly to make the inexpensive meal extra special. She set the table with loving care and everyone loved it.

After dinner, the family gathered around the tree. One by one they opened their simple gifts. In peace and love they gazed at their Christmas treasures.

Years passed. Every Christmas the children spoke affectionately of that special, wonderful Christmas where less became more—the best Christmas ever.

"DON'T WAIT TO SAY YOU LOVE ME"

Don't wait to say you love me,
Don't wait to sing my song.
Be quick to let me know;
I may not be here long.
    Don't think there's still tomorrow,
    Do something nice today.
    In life's most hectic hour
    Love must find a way.

Let me know you love me,
Show me that you care.
While the clock is ticking
Keep me in your prayer.
    Don't wait to show you love me,
    Don't let the present fly.
    Build now the loving memories
    Before life passes by.

TOO BUSY OR TO-GETHER?

Derek kept a well-planned schedule, completed studies to upgrade his teaching status, sang in the choir, assisted the youth director and felt pleased with his achievements. Yet the feeling that something wasn't just right bothered him.

Derek's dad had called the previous night and asked if Derek could make it home for Christmas Eve so the family could attend the church service together.

"Sorry, Dad. I have a schedule up to my ears and will be busy preparing for the youth play on Christmas Day." He hung up, remembering the Bible spoke of putting family first. What should he do? Finally an idea came. He called several older teens to help with play preparations ahead of time. He reworked his schedule, decided not to call and prepared to surprise his family.

On Christmas Eve, Derek drove straight to the candlelit church. Christmas sacredness lingered in the softly glowing sanctuary. Derek anxiously glanced around. His parents huddled in a pew near the front. "Room for one more?" he whispered. Dad and Mom looked thrilled.

Then Derek glanced at a banner near the pulpit: *Christmas is made for us to love one another.* Glad he came, Derek asked God's forgiveness and vowed nothing was as important as putting his parents at the top of his busy schedule.

BOXES AND LIGHTS

Our family had been separated for three months; my husband Bob had taken a job in the Seattle area where we could be closer to our parents. I remained in Spokane with our four sons until our house sold and we closed on our new place.

How we longed to all be together in our new home before Christmas! We hurriedly finished our last-minute packing, made the precarious drive over the mountains and finally arrived "home." After we fed the tired, hungry boys, we curled up in sleeping bags on the rugs.

The next day was Christmas Eve. I hung a treasured picture in the living room so the house would become home. I'd carefully packed the decorations in separately marked boxes, but in vain. Bob and the boys searched and searched for a real Christmas tree; all had been sold out. Discouraged, I drew a hot bath, soaked and prayed for a long time.

When I came out, decorations adorned the living room. Lights twinkled. A charming artificial tree stood in front of the window. One husband and four sons all wore big grins. We gathered around the tree, sang "Silent Night," and thanked God we could be together for Christmas. The stacks of boxes faded. The lights brightened. The air filled with laughter, for God had blessed our family.

THE FIRST NOEL

The first Noel the angel did say
Was to certain poor shepherds in fields as they
   lay;
In fields where they lay tending their sheep,
On a cold winter's night that was so deep.

Refrain:
Noel, Noel, Noel, Noel,
Born is the King of Israel.

They looked up and saw a star
Shining in the east, beyond them far;
And to the earth it gave great light,
And so it continued both day and night.

Refrain

And by the light of that same star
Three Wise Men came from country far;
To seek for a King was their intent,
And to follow the star wherever it went.

Refrain

This star drew nigh to the northwest,
Over Bethlehem it took its rest;
And there it did both stop and stay,
Right over the place where Jesus lay.

Refrain

Then entered in those Wise Men three,
Full reverently upon the knee,
And offered there, in His presence,
Their gold and myrrh and frankincense.

Refrain

Then let us all with one accord
Sing praises to our heavenly Lord;
That hath made heaven and earth of naught,
And with His blood mankind hath bought.

Refrain

Words & Music: Traditional English carol,
possibly dating from as early as the
thirteenth century.

GOD REST YE MERRY, GENTLEMEN

God rest ye merry, gentlemen, let nothing you
    dismay,
Remember Christ our Savior was born on
    Christmas Day;
To save us all from Satan's power when we
    were gone astray.

Refrain:

O tidings of comfort and joy, comfort and joy;
O tidings of comfort and joy.

In Bethlehem, in Israel, this blessed Babe was
    born,
And laid within a manger upon this blessed
    morn;
The which His mother Mary did nothing take
    in scorn.

Refrain

From God our heavenly Father a blessed angel
    came;
And unto certain shepherds brought tidings of
    the same;
How that in Bethlehem was born the Son of
    God by name.

Refrain

"Fear not, then," said the angel, "Let nothing
   you afright
This day is born a Savior of a pure Virgin
   bright,
To free all those who trust in Him from Satan's
   power and might."

Refrain

Now to the Lord sing praises all you within
   this place,
And with true love and brotherhood each
   other now embrace;
This holy tide of Christmas all others doth
   deface.

Refrain

   Words & Music: Traditional English Carol

"HARK!
THE HERALD ANGELS SING"

Hark! The herald angels sing,
"Glory to the newborn King,
Peace on earth, and mercy mild,
God and sinners reconciled."
Joyful, all ye nations, rise,
Join the triumph of the skies;
With the angel host proclaim,
"Christ is born in Bethlehem!"

CHARLES WESLEY, 1707–1788

HYMN NOTES

When we sing "Hark, the Herald Angels Sing" we are singing a song written more than 250 years ago, by a man who wrote over six thousand hymns!

Charles Wesley was born in England in 1707, four years after his brother John, who started the Methodist church. Both became ministers. Charles wrote so many hymns people called him the "hymn writer of the ages."

When Charles accepted Jesus into his heart, he told a friend about it. He asked his friend, "Should I keep still and not tell others how wonderful I feel?"

"No!" said his friend. "If you had ten thousand tongues, you should use them all for Jesus." Impressed with the good advice, Wesley sat down and wrote:

> Oh, for a thousand tongues to sing,
> My great Redeemer's praise,
> The glories of my God and King,
> The triumphs of His grace!

The next time you sing "Hark! The Herald Angels Sing," remember Charles Wesley, who praised God by writing hymns.

ANGEL IN BLUE JEANS

The church program was ready to begin. Costumed children stood in their places, ready to tell the age-old Christmas story. Mary, Joseph, baby Jesus, angels, and shepherds nervously waited, as did patient parents. What could be holding things up?

A rustle came from the back of the sanctuary. Ten-year-old Ginger Adams dashed down the aisle and up to the platform. She wore ragged blue jeans and her flaming ponytail flipped behind her. Ginger frantically clutched the curtains until she finally found a way through. The audience rippled with laughter.

Ginger came from a poverty-level family. Her mother seldom attended church and no one knew where the father was. The ten-year-old girl never wore a dress. She said she wanted to be comfortable, but others knew she had no nice clothes.

The curtain opened and the nativity story began. The play progressed smoothly. At the end, Ginger stepped forward, jeans hidden by her angel costume. Her wings hung awkwardly; a halo lay precariously on her bright red ponytail. Floppy-soled, too-big tennis shoes stuck out from under her white robe.

Ginger turned to face the baby Jesus. In a

soprano voice sweet and clear, she reverently began the carol, "Away in a Manger." Mrs. Adams, who had slipped in unnoticed, sat quietly in the back row, wearing a pleased smile.

Ginger stopped and gulped. "I–I love You, Jesus," she stammered. "I–I love You because You love me." She gazed at the star above the manger and resumed her song: "I love Thee, Lord Jesus, look down from the sky."

Christmas season became something extra special that night for all in the church and the red-headed angel in blue jeans glowed with love.

Be not forgetful to entertain strangers: for thereby some have entertained angels unawares (HEBREWS 13:2).

If we knew Jesus planned to spend Christmas with us, preparations wouldn't stop with house cleaning. We can feel the Presence of Jesus in our homes always, especially this time of year, if we stop, look, and listen.

Prepare for Him. Shop, bake, and decorate early. Don't let the birthday of God's Son get lost in wrapping paper and ribbon. Go caroling with families and friends. Retell the story of a wondrous night two thousand years ago that changed history. You'll change the holidays into what they should be: a "holy-day" season filled with love, joy, peace and gladness.

It Came Upon
the Midnight Clear

It came upon the midnight clear, that glorious
    song of old,
From angels bending near the earth, to touch
    their harps of gold;
"Peace on the earth, good will to men, from
    heaven's all gracious King."
The world in solemn stillness lay, to hear the
    angels sing.
Still through the cloven skies they come with
    peaceful wings unfurled,
And still their heavenly music floats over all
    the weary world;
Above its sad and lowly plains, they bend on
    hovering wing,
And ever over its Babel sounds the blessed
    angels sing.
But with the woes of sin and strife the world
    has suffered long;
Beneath the angel strain have rolled two
    thousand years of wrong;
And man, at war with man, hears not the love
    song which they bring;
O hush the noise, ye men of strife and hear
    the angels sing.

And ye, beneath life's crushing load, whose
  forms are bending low,
Who toil along the climbing way with painful
  steps and slow,
Look now! for glad and golden hours come
  swiftly on the wing.
O rest beside the weary road, and hear the
  angels sing!
For lo! the days are hastening on, by prophet
  seen of old,
When with the ever circling years shall come
  the time foretold
When peace shall over all the earth its ancient
  splendors fling,
And the whole world send back the song
  which now the angels sing.

EDMUND HAMILTON SEARS, 1849

FROM A STABLE TO A TRAILER

Bitter, chilling wind gusts shook the tiny trailer from which the church youth group and parents worked selling Christmas trees to help finance a mission trip to Mexico. They had committed themselves to volunteer a week's work and try to win souls for the Lord. Tonight was another fund-raiser.

Dave burst in. "Yes!" he cheered. "I sold three trees." Corrie smiled at her son, shivered, and wished she were home. Stacks of unmailed cards and decorations needing to be put up haunted her. As the night wore on, and fewer persons came to buy trees during their shift, Dave fell asleep on a couch. Doubts rose and Corrie prayed, "Lord, please show me our efforts will be blessed."

A shadow moved across the window. A drifting cloud exposed the round silver moon and a lone, bright star that reminded Corrie of the Star of Bethlehem. "Did Mary and Joseph wonder what You had in mind for them?" she prayed. "I can't even comprehend Your sacrifice." Shame filled her and her tears blurred the star. "This is nothing compared with what You did for us."

Dave stirred and stretched. "You okay, Mom?"

"Just fine. I hear another customer. My turn to go." She stepped into the night air. "Happy birthday, Jesus—and thank You."

THE TINY MANGER SCENE

The family gathered for Christmas, but only outwardly. Hurt feelings lingered from years past. Touchy attitudes and snide remarks filled the air with contempt. No one could find the peace so desperately longed for and needed.

Aunt Susan quietly peeled potatoes in the kitchen, tears dripping. *Please, Lord, do something to heal the bad feelings in my family,* she silently prayed.

More unkind words burst forth. Then ever so quietly a lilting tune rang forth from the background: "Silent Night! Holy Night."

Conversation halted. Everyone turned. A small child had wound a nativity music box. Round and round the scene turned. Carol after glorious carol sounded. The little girl gazed up at her family with pleading eyes. Someone started singing. Others blended in. Arms wrapped around shoulders and waists. "I'm sorry" mingled with sobs and laughter as the healing Spirit of Christmas filled the home.

Uncle Mac hugged each and advised, "Let go, kids, and start from here. Love each other the way Jesus loves you."

Aunt Susan placed the pan of potatoes on the stove, wiped her eyes and smiled. "All is calm," she joined in, "all is bright. . ."

"Silent Night! Holy Night!"

Silent night! Holy night!
All is calm, all is bright
Round yon virgin mother and Child!
Holy Infant, so tender and mild,
Sleep in heavenly peace;
Sleep in heavenly peace.

Joseph Mohr (1792–1848)

HYMN NOTES

Naughty mice and a terrible snowstorm led to our best-loved Christmas carol, "Silent Night! Holy Night!" On Christmas Eve in 1818, far away in the Bavarian village of Oberndorf, Joseph Mohr and Franz Gruber looked at each other in despair. Mice had crawled inside the old church organ and it wouldn't play until it could be repaired.

They stared out the window into thick snow that made travel to get someone to repair the organ impossible. What could they do? Christmas services without music would be dull and lifeless.

Franz sadly turned away but Joseph continued to watch the snow-covered village, praying for God's help. Gradually the blizzard lessened and left a beautiful, peaceful night. Words came into Joseph's heart and mind, "Silent Night! Holy Night!"

The next morning he handed what he had written to Franz. Before long, Franz hummed a simple tune—but the organ still would not work.

That night in a small, candlelit church, the villagers heard the new carol, sung with Franz Gruber playing the melody in chords on his guitar.

THE LITTLE SLIDE

I spotted the wooden indoor slide at a garage sale. It stood about three feet tall, just right for two of my little grandsons. I visualized it in bright colors: red, yellow, blue. I jiggled the slide. It needed to be tightened a bit. A small smile crept across my face.

"Dad," I said, after reaching home and calling him on the phone. "How would you like to go in together on a wooden slide for the grandsons?" I described it enthusiastically. "I'll buy the paint and supplies if you'll do the tightening and painting. How 'bout it?"

Dad didn't hesitate for a minute. Weeks went by. Dad went all out fixing up the slide. He glued and painted and glued again, doing it all indoors with the windows open. The fumes irritated his lungs so badly he was sick for a long time afterward. His gift showed a true labor of love.

The grandkids were delighted with their present. They spent many, many hours on the slide until they wore it out.

Thank you, Dad, for that project and many others you have worked on in love throughout all the years.

Anita

CHRISTMAS AROUND THE TREE

*O give thanks unto the LORD,
for he is good.*
PSALM 106:1

When I met the Donihues, they automatically made me a part of their family. That was simply the way they were. Everyone who entered their home felt welcome.

I'll never forget my first Christmas Eve with them. We gathered around the tree and Dad (Brother Donihue, back then) opened his Bible. All four of his teenage sons sat reverently while he read the Christmas story. Mom sat near him, face shining with love. We sang a Christmas hymn and thanked God for giving us His Son. It only took a few moments, but meant so much.

I didn't know at the time I would one day marry one of those sons. I did know that was the kind of Christmas I wanted someday with my own husband and children.

Thank you, Dad and Mom, for that first special Christmas Eve and the family tradition that is being passed down through generations.

Anita

"O HOLY NIGHT"

O holy night, the stars are brightly shining;
It is the night of the dear Savior's birth!
Long lay the world in sin and error pining,
Till He appeared and the soul felt its worth.
A thrill of hope, the weary soul rejoices,
For yonder breaks a new and glorious morn.

Refrain:
Fall on your knees, O hear the angel voices!
O night divine, O night when Christ was born!
O night, O holy night, O night divine!

Led by the light of faith serenely beaming,
With glowing hearts by His cradle we stand.
So led by light of a star sweetly gleaming,
Here came the wise men from Orient land.
The King of kings lay thus in lowly manger,
In all our trials born to be our friend!

Refrain:
Fall on your knees, O hear the angel voices!
O night divine, O night when Christ was born!
O night, O holy night, O night divine!

Truly He taught us to love one another;
His law is love and His gospel is peace.
Chains shall He break for the slave is our brother.
And in His Name all oppression shall cease.
Sweet hymns of joy in grateful chorus raise we,
Let all within us praise His holy Name!

Refrain:
Fall on your knees, O hear the angel voices!
O night divine, O night when Christ was born!
O night, O holy night, O night divine!

PLACIDE CLAPPEAU, 1847; translated from
French to English by John Sullivan Dwight,
1812–1893

"O LITTLE TOWN OF BETHLEHEM"

O little town of Bethlehem,
How still we see thee lie!
Above thy deep and dreamless sleep
The silent stars go by;
Yet in thy dark streets shineth
The everlasting Light;
The hopes and fears of all the years
Are met in thee tonight.

PHILLIPS BROOKS (1835–1893)

HYMN NOTES

Phillips Brooks had a dream. More than anything in the world, he wanted to be in Bethlehem on Christmas Eve and see where Jesus was born. Yet many years passed before his dream came true. America was fighting the Civil War and Phillips could not go. He served God as a minister and continued to dream. At last he walked the land where Jesus walked so long ago. What joy he felt, more than he had thought possible.

Years later, Phillips wanted to write a Christmas hymn for the children of his church. He remembered the wonderful Christmas Eve when he visited the Holy Land. Words formed in his mind, and he wrote the words to the carol we sing over 125 years later: "O Little Town of Bethlehem."

The story doesn't end there. Phillips needed the words set to music. He asked the church organist to help. Lewis Redner tried and tried, but nothing sounded right. Discouraged, he went to bed one night. When he awakened, the whole melody rang in his mind. He quickly wrote it down.

How wonderful to remember, as Phillips Brooks did, that shepherds knelt and angels sang in Bethlehem the night Jesus was born.

TOPPING THE TREE

Pastor Jenson stepped to the pulpit. The congregation seemed distracted that morning. He knew it came from Christmas excitement.

"Today I wish to speak of how holidays can divide a family," he announced. He named a variety of things that caused stress and arguments of what should be a blessed time of the year.

He walked to the living tree near the church platform. The tree had no decorations except a shining star on the top. Pastor Jenson proceeded to hang pictures cut from magazines on the branches: a mother; a father; a teen; a child; a baby; grandparents; aunts and uncles and cousins.

He paused and turned to his questioning congregation. "Families have a choice, to focus on the holidays or on Jesus Christ. I ask you to lift your gaze to the top of the tree." He carefully hung a picture of Jesus in front of the star. "Whether your tree has a star, an angel, or lights, think of Christ as the head of your family and your holidays."

Pastor Jenson moved his arms in the shape of a triangle with the tips of his fingers pointing upward, then pointed to the picture of Jesus. "The closer you draw to Christ," he said, "the closer your family draws together."

"WHAT CAN I GIVE HIM?"

What can I give Him,
    Poor as I am?
If I were a shepherd
    I would bring a lamb.
If I were a Wise Man
    I would do my part—
Yet what can I give Him,
    Give my heart.

CHRISTINA GEORGINA ROSETTI (1830–1894)

CARRIE'S CRADLE

Lynn adoringly watched her granddaughter Carrie Lynn excitedly open her Christmas gift. The small girl's dark eyes, so much like her grandmother's, sparkled. Carrie Lynn had looked forward to this gift for two whole years. Each Christmas, Lynn told her, "Wait until you are seven. I want you to take good care of it."

Now the child eagerly tore away the wrappings. She exposed a lovely doll cradle with pink and blue hearts painted on the sides. The handcarved semicircular base had been carefully painted baby blue.

Carrie Lynn threw her arms around her grandma's neck and climbed onto her lap. "Thank you, Grandma! Tell me the story again, please."

Lynn settled back, rocking her granddaughter. "The Christmas I turned seven, I wanted a cradle for my baby doll more than anything. Oh, how I prayed for a cradle. Mother and Daddy earned their living by farming. It had been a hard year and they had little money. Every night for two weeks, I heard them whispering after I went to bed. Sometimes I heard a light *tap, tap, tap.*

"Christmas morning came. I awoke and found the beautiful cradle under our tree. Daddy and Mother made it from parts of apple boxes and painted it, just like it is today. The cradle has always been my treasure. Since I had no girls, I waited for you to come along. Now, my love, it's yours to keep."

"Tell me again about the baby Jesus, please Grandma," Carrie Lynn pleaded.

Her grandmother smiled. "That same Christmas I learned baby Jesus was born in a simple manger. God gave me a special gift. Because of Jesus' love, I asked Him into my heart and became His little child."

"I'm His child, too, aren't I?" She bounced on Lynn's knee.

"Yes, you are, and He loves you."

Carrie Lynn slid from her grandma's lap. She lovingly tucked her baby doll into her new cradle of great treasure. She kissed her doll and whispered, "I love Jesus. I love Grandma. And I love you."

"REJOICE, REJOICE, YE CHRISTIANS"

Rejoice, rejoice, ye Christians, with all your
    heart this morn!
O hear the blessèd tidings, the Lord, the Christ
    is born,
Now brought us by the angels that stand about
    God's throne;
O lovely are the voices that make such tidings
    known!
O hearken to their singing! This Child shall be
    your Friend;
The Father so hath willed it, that thus your
    woes should end.
The Son is freely given, that in Him ye may
    have
The Father's grace and blessing, and know He
    loves to save.
Nor deem the form too lowly that clothes Him
    at this hour;
For know ye what it hideth? 'Tis God's
    almighty power.
Though now within the manger so poor and
    weak He lies,
He is the Lord of all things, He reigns above
    the skies.

GEISTLICHE LIEDER

CHRISTMAS BRINGS JOY
TO EVERY HEART

Christmas brings joy to every heart,
  Sets old and young rejoicing,
What angels sang once to all on earth,
  Oh, hear the children voicing.
Bright is the tree with lights aglow,
  Like birds that perch together,
The child that holdeth Christmas dear
  Shall keep these joys forever.
Joy comes to the all the world today,
  To halls and cottage hasting,
Come, sparrow and dove, from roof tree tall,
  And share our Christmas feasting.
Dance, little child, on mother's knee,
  The lovely day is dawning,
The road to paradise is found
  The blessèd Christmas morning.

BERNHARDT SEVERIN INGEMANN

THE STAR LADY

A happy heart makes the face cheerful.
PROVERBS 15:13, NIV

Snow fell. Roads became slick. Heather hurried into the local post office to mail last-minute packages. She cringed when she walked through the door. Last Christmas she'd been served by a "bah humbug" clerk. *He must have been very tired,* she reassured herself. *Christmas isn't easy for postal workers.*

Heather rounded the bend in the long line of customers, and before long her turn came to be helped. A short young lady with multi-colored framed glasses and a pen behind one ear greeted her warmly. After Heather paid the postage and deposited her packages, the lady asked her to wait a moment. She reached into a nearby basket and gave Heather a handmade foil star.

"Why—thank you," Heather stammered. "It's nice of you to go to the trouble."

"It gives me energy to see people happy." The clerk beamed. "Merry Christmas!"

When Heather reached the door to leave, she looked back. Each customer greeted the postal clerk: some serious; some grumpy; a few wearing smiles. But all left smiling, clutching their handmade stars.

"O COME, ALL YE FAITHFUL"

O come, all ye faithful, joyful and triumphant,
O come ye, O come ye to Bethlehem;
Come and behold Him, born the King of
   angels:
O come, let us adore Him, O come let us
   adore Him,
O come, let us adore Him, Christ the Lord.

ANONYMOUS

HYMN NOTES

No one knows when or by whom "O Come, All Ye Faithful" was written. According to legend, this hymn was probably written in the thirteenth century. At that time, churches first began using manger scenes to honor Christmas and Jesus' birth. Now, about seven hundred years later, the carol is sung in over 120 languages by millions of faithful Christians all over the world.

"INFANT HOLY, INFANT LOWLY"

Infant holy, Infant lowly, for His bed a cattle
stall;
Oxen lowing, little knowing, Christ the Babe
is Lord of all.
Swift are winging angels singing, noels ring-
ing, tidings bringing:
Christ the Babe is Lord of all.

Flocks were sleeping, shepherds keeping vigil
till the morning new
Saw the glory, heard the story, tidings of a
gospel true.
Thus rejoicing, free from sorrow, praises
voicing, greet the morrow:
Christ the Babe was born for you.

Words: Traditional carol;
translated from Polish to English by
EDITH MARGARET GELLIBRAND REED, 1925.

DEAR LITTLE STRANGER

Low in a manger, dear little Stranger,
Jesus, the wonderful Savior, was born.
There was none to receive Him, none to
  believe Him,
None but the angels were watching that morn.

Refrain:
Dear little Stranger, slept in a manger,
No downy pillow under His head;
But with the poor He slumbered secure,
The dear little Babe in His bed.

Angels descending, over Him bending,
Chanted a tender and silent refrain;
Then a wonderful story told of His glory,
Unto the shepherds on Bethlehem's plain.

Refrain

Dear little Stranger, born in a manger,
Maker and Monarch, and Savior of all;
I will love You forever! Grieve You? No, never!
You did for me make Your bed in a stall.

CHARLES HUTCHINSON GABRIEL

I LOVE TO HEAR THE STORY

I love to hear the story which angel voices
    tell,
How once the King of glory came down on
    earth to dwell.
I am both weak and sinful; but this I surely
    know,
The Lord came down to save me, because He
    loved me so.
I'm glad my blessèd Savior was once a child
    like me,
To show how pure and holy His little ones
    might be;
And, if I try to follow His footsteps here
    below,
He never will forget me, because He loves
    me so.

EMILY HUNTINGTON MILLER

A NEW AND DIFFERENT CHRISTMAS

God blessed our family by permitting Mom to live until she was almost ninety-six. Single, I lived at home until after Dad died, then bought a home where she lived with me: editor, mentor, best friend. We both loved Christmas and shared fifty-six wonderful holiday seasons baking, decorating, selecting gifts, attending Christmas concerts and church services.

December 1992 arrived. I'd been alone since August, adjusting to "me" instead of "we" with the help of a loving God, caring family, and a multitude of supportive friends. I decorated early as usual, watched old and new Christmas specials, hummed carols and joyously celebrated Christ's birth, also as usual. The Christmas Eve candlelight service brought tears when we passed the flame from candle to candle; it had been Mom's favorite service of the year. But the quick encircling arm of a young alto next to me in choir brought comfort.

I awakened early Christmas morning. A few hours later, our family would meet for our traditional dinner and open gifts. Depression such as I hadn't experienced for weeks settled over me. All the joy of the season fled.

When it got light enough, I bundled up and walked to the bluff about a half mile from home, pelting along at just under a gallop. A couple miles of brisk walking and talking with God always brought the healing peace I needed.

That morning, it did not. I felt torn apart. I'd already learned the "firsts" were the worst. First visit to our family doctor. First trip to a favorite restaurant. Once done, it never bothered me again. Now I faced my first Christmas without Mom.

"I can't do it," I cried in the crisp, cold air. "I can't go to my brother's home where we've had so many happy times." Yet what if I didn't? Each of my family also had to face this first Christmas. I couldn't spoil everyone else's day by staying home. I gave in. "All right, Lord, I'll go, but it will have to be in Your strength, not mine. I don't have any." I waited for a surge of that badly needed strength. It didn't come. Sighing, I headed for home.

I can't remember how many times I repeated my talisman, "Not my strength, but Yours." The last was when I rang the doorbell at my brother's, still wondering how to handle what lay ahead. I stepped inside—and into a new and different Christmas. My sister-in-law had considerately planned a menu far from the traditional "Grandma's favorite." Carol singing and gift opening were altered. A flood of gladness washed away my dread and brought peace.

Are you facing "a new and different Christmas" due to death, divorce, or too many miles between? Cling to Philippians 4:13: "I can do all things through Christ which strengtheneth me." You really can, just as I did.

"I HEARD THE BELLS ON CHRISTMAS DAY"

I heard the bells on Christmas Day
Their old familiar carols play,
And wild and sweet the words repeat
Of peace on earth, good will to men.

HENRY W. LONGFELLOW (1807–1882)

Inspirational Library

Beautiful purse/pocket-size editions of Christian classics bound in flexible leatherette. These books make thoughtful gifts for everyone on your list, including yourself!

When I'm on My Knees   The highly popular collection of devotional thoughts on prayer, especially for women.
Flexible Leatherette $4.97

The Bible Promise Book   Over 1,000 promises from God's Word arranged by topic. What does God promise about matters like: Anger, Illness, Jealousy, Love, Money, Old Age, and Mercy? Find out in this book!
Flexible Leatherette $3.97

Daily Wisdom for Women   A daily devotional for women seeking biblical wisdom to apply to their lives. Scripture taken from the New American Standard Version of the Bible.
Flexible Leatherette $4.97

My Daily Prayer Journal   Each page is dated and features a Scripture verse and ample room for you to record your thoughts, prayers, and praises. One page for each day of the year.
Flexible Leatherette $4.97

Available wherever books are sold.
Or order from:

Barbour Publishing, Inc.
P.O. Box 719
Uhrichsville, OH 44683
http://www.barbourbooks.com

If you order by mail add $2.00 to your order for shipping.
Prices subject to change without notice.